pool builder
MARKETING **PROS**

DIVE INTO

ONLINE MARKETING

A GUIDE FOR POOL CONTRACTORS

By Pool Builder Marketing PROS

Sean Charsley & Josh Brisbane

"We pride ourselves on providing the best digital marketing services for Pool Builders while maintaining our core values. We are extremely focused as well as the hardest working agency on getting the most ROI out of your marketing dollars. With our experience and eagerness to work with new clients it would be great to talk to you and see how we can take your brand to the next level."

TABLE OF CONTENTS

CHAPTER 1
INTRODUCTION

HI, if you're reading this book you must be curious about online marketing for your Pool business. Chances are you've dabbled with online or digital marketing in the past and maybe didn't see the results you wanted. Or you hired one of those large generalized digital marketing companies that promised you the world only to keep cashing your checks with no real growth or return on your investment. Unfortunately, in today's digital age anyone with a laptop can portray themselves as a digital marketer. We at **Pool Builder Marketing PROS** only focus on one thing and one thing only. Working with Pool Builders to get them REAL results and a true return on your investment dollars.

A little about us and why you should want to work with us.

Pool Builder Marketing Pros is the combined creation of Josh Brisbane and Sean Charsley. Both with extensive backgrounds in Digital Marketing. Their passion for everything H2O and design made the pool industry the perfect fit.

Sean Charsley – Co-Founder of Pool Builder Marketing Pros
Sean's background in marketing began with the iconic brands such as The Hard Rock Hotel, Hakkasan Nightclub, and The Golden Nugget Hotel & Casino. In the hospitality industry, his main objective was to create strategies on how to increase clientele foot traffic and persuade them to visit his establishments.

With the highly competitive Las Vegas market, Sean became an expert in digital as well as traditional marketing.

Sean's career success transitioned him into the online consulting industry.

Here he focuses 100% of his efforts on increasing customer traffic and conversion rates for Pool Builders. He became an expert on how to capture an audience and influence them to produce sales.

Josh Brisbane – Co-Founder of Pool Builder Marketing Pros

Josh's passion for digital marketing can be traced back to working for such prominent brands Coca-Cola and Evian Water. Allowing him to gain the experience of how the big corporations marketing initiatives operate.

Being a business owner for over 10 years. Whether securing new clients for his marketing business or building a social media presence for his lifestyle brand, Josh has been in the digital marketing game from the start.

The reason? We enjoy helping businesses grow, by increasing their client base and by expanding their brand exposure.

Josh has taken his over 10 years' experience of building his own brands and co-created **Pool Builder Marketing Pros** with Sean to help Pool Builders expand their business.

Outside of Pool Builder Marketing Pros, Josh is a family man at heart. He enjoys the beach life with his wife, son and two Golden Retrievers. He is an avid surfer, a student of Krav Maga and a fitness buff who likes to stay active.

As a VP of Membership for his local Toastmasters club he is always trying to improve his Spanish speaking skills for his Cabo trips.

Together Josh and Sean started **Pool Builder Marketing PROS** with a goal. To get Pool Builders more leads so that they can build more pools. This goal will also help to generate more jobs in our economy and within the swimming pool industry as a whole.

"DIVE INTO ONLINE MARKETING" – A GUIDE FOR SWIMMING POOL CONTRACTORS is the roadmap to successfully marketing your pool business online. The Internet is the perfect tool for marketing and advertising your pool builder business, and if we look back over the last decade the way consumers looked for your services was via the telephone book or Newspaper. Back then you had to have your business listed there mainly because all your competitors did and that's the place your customers went to find what they were looking for.

When it comes to Internet marketing for Pool Builders there are a number of avenues and channels to explore. In this book we will touch briefly on the different online marketing channels that are available for you and then go more into depth on each throughout the book.

This book has been written for the Swimming Pool Contractor, with little to no Online Marketing experience. This book will show you the importance of your online presence and how to put it all together. We want to give you an Online Marketing plan of your own or give you the knowledge so you can be educated when working with a Digital Marketing company.

Chapter 1 Key Points

- Sean & Josh have years of experience and are eager to help
- Pool Builder Marketing Pros main goal is to provide you with quality leads that convert to sales through digital marketing strategies and tactics
- This book is a guide and a must read if you own a Pool Building or Pool Service company

ENJOY!

CHAPTER 2

WHY IS INTERNET MARKETING SO IMPORTANT IN TODAY'S DAY AND AGE?

Online marketing isn't something new for pool businesses to consider anymore. In fact, it's quite the opposite...having been going on for years now and seemingly has no end in sight. Yet, far too many pool business owners neglect how important online marketing is for their business success. Among the reasons this seems to be is time. Another money. And yet another is that they just don't care. The reality is; however, customers do care and in order to be relevant in today's crowded marketplace, being online is a <u>MUST</u>.

Almost 4.57 billion people were active internet users as of July 2020. With an estimated one in four Americans making at least one online purchase a week, 70% of Facebook users interacting with Facebook daily and the average American now checks their phones 96 times a day – that's once every 10 minutes, according to new research by global tech care company Asurion. That's a 20% daily increase from a similar survey conducted by Asurion just two years ago.

There are countless reasons that being online is not just important - but rather a must when it comes to connecting with consumers. It's valuable to consider investing some of your hard-earned money into online marketing so that you can gain easy to use, automated online marketing solutions. This will allow you to spend more time doing what you do best... BUILD MORE POOLS, make more money and create more jobs.

Think of your online marketing as an automatic money machine. If someone had a machine that was selling $100 bills for $20, how many would you buy? Would you only buy 10 because your budget was only $200? NO, you would buy as many as you possibly could. Think of online marketing the same way. With technology now, marketing doesn't have to be a gamble like a Vegas slot machine. We can now measure and track every lead that comes in, what works and what doesn't so that your ROI on you marketing efforts continues to grow. Online marketing is like a water faucet. You can turn it on full blast when you need some business now to get you through the slower months. You can turn down the pressure during the spring and summer months when you're already slammed.

Why would you choose to postpone putting time and effort into your digital marketing? Different business owners may come up with a variety of reasons to avoid this form of marketing, but in the end, you're just postponing the inevitable if you want to stay in business for long.

Some businesses owners believe that they don't have the time or the money to be competitive online. They think they can only face so many projects at once and they are still dealing with the ins and outs of the business in general. Many of them may prefer to take things slowly and to stick with one or two basic forms of advertising, assuming that their business will evolve as time passes.

They may even think the best strategy is simply to wait for customers to show up via word of mouth. This is not an effective approach to growing or even sustaining your business. There is never a guarantee that your business will attract customers just by existing and even if it does, you may not attract as many customers as you need to make your business stay profitable. With cost of goods going up, labor rates increasing, you need to maximize your profitability just to stay afloat in the coming years.

If you have been avoiding digital marketing, is it because you think you are simply not ready? Or do you think you just need some time to grow and then you will figure out the digital marketing angle down the road?

The problem with this approach is that your potential customers are already online. Right now!! Most likely staring at their phones looking at pictures of pools wishing they had one. There's a good chance they might already be looking for a Pool Builder in your service area but if they can't find you easily, they are probably going to choose one of your competitors. This is how people do business today. When someone has an interest in getting a pool put in, whether it is in your area or in general or if they are just curious about your brand, the first thing they are going to do is research online and see what they can find out about you.

They expect to find you there with a beautiful website and a strong social media presence. They may be looking for reviews so they can learn what other people are saying about your company and whether you are going to be their future pool builder. If a potential customer can't find you online, they may conclude that your business doesn't appear to be legitimate. There is a very good chance that a lot of these prospects may decide not to take your business seriously and they will quickly head somewhere else. Once they have made that decision, they probably won't be back. That's just the facts.

For your Pool business to be successful, you need to pay attention to what your competitors are doing and learn from them. Think of your competitors as not just someone that you want to beat, but as people who have something to teach you. When you look at what your competitors are doing, you will get some idea of what is working and what isn't working.

Most likely, your competitors have established a strong web presence. What kind of content are they using? Are they blogging, or are they using a lot of photos and videos? How do they communicate their brand and what makes them unique? How well do they engage with their audience? Do you think you can do better? You can't if you don't participate in competing in the digital world.

If your prospects begin to search for a pool company similar to yours and are able to find your competitors' website but not yours, your business is not even in the running. Your prospects can't choose you if they don't know about you. In this scenario, your competitors have just beat you.

Your potential and future customer are online, it's a great opportunity for you to reach leads that are looking for your business. There are billions of people online just waiting to find your company. They're constantly conducting searches to find relevant information about Pools, Landscaping Design, Backyard Ideas, etc.

By investing in your online presence, you're helping your company reach those interested leads. Even if you only operate locally, your audience is online. Online marketing is valuable to your business, it helps you get connected to leads that are most interested in your product. With online marketing you can now personalize your marketing efforts and customize your audience's experience. You can create a tailored experience that best fits their interests. It's good to create multiple, personalized marketing pieces over just creating one generalized ad. The ability to personalize, track, and measure your marketing strategy is why online marketing is so important to your business in todays world. It helps you deliver a better experience for your leads, which turns them into customers.

Online marketing is so important because it helps you drive more qualified traffic and you reach more leads that are actually interested in your business. You can target leads specifically by different characteristics. Online marketing allows you to target by demographic information, median household income, interests, hobbies, and even spending habits. These days you can get very precise with your targeting to ensure you're only reaching leads you know will be interested and that can actually afford to get a pool put in.

With Online marketing you are exposing your business to billions of people 24 hrs. a day 7 days a week. When people are more familiar with your business, they are more likely to choose you when they are ready for that dream pool.

Online marketing is extremely cost effective. One of the best parts about online marketing is that is affordable and drives a good return on your investment. When you are investing back into your business, you want a good ROI right? Well with technology and the right marketing strategy that's what you get. With the ability to target the people that are more interested and have the means to buy a pool, online marketing is the best thing you could do for the future of your business. With online marketing you can measure the analytics of each of your campaigns. The days of guessing to see if anyone saw your ads are over. Analytics allow you to see the different metrics of your ads and see how well they are performing in real time.

If you still feel that Online marketing isn't for you then keep reading to learn more. If you're sold on the wonders of online marketing and don't want to waste any more valuable time sitting on the fence. You can contact at us at www.PoolBuilderMarketingPROS.com We can help!

Chapter 2 Key Points

- Far too many pool business owners neglect how important online marketing is for their business' success
- It's valuable to consider investing some of your hard-earned money into online marketing so that you can gain easy to use, automated online marketing solutions.

- With technology now, marketing doesn't have to be a gamble like a Vegas slot machine. We can now measure and track every lead that comes in, what works and what doesn't so that your ROI on you marketing efforts continues to grow.

- There's a good chance they might already be looking for a Pool Builder in your service area but if they can't find you easily, they are probably going to choose one of your competitors.

- Online marketing is so important because it helps you drive more qualified traffic and you reach more leads that are actually interested in your business

- With Online marketing you are exposing your business to billions of people 24 hrs. a day 7 days a week.

Chapter 3
YOUR WEBSITE IS YOUR ONLINE PRESENCE FOUNDATION

A great looking website is very important for your industry. They say a picture is worth a thousand words. Well in the Pool industry a picture of a beautiful pool could turn into millions of dollars in your pocket. Your company's website is often your first impression you give to potential customers and helps to establish credibility. Customers will see it and immediately form an opinion about your business based on nothing more than how it looks and operates. I've been on thousands of websites that I've gotten to only to be disappointed at the look, feel, and functionality of the site. Luckily for me, a company having a terrible website saves me a fortune because I don't stick around long enough to buy anything. Sadly, though for that business they continue to lose visitors (and money) daily. It's always disappointing to see a company spend the money to drive traffic to their site only to have people be unimpressed and leave after only a few seconds. In today's world of instant gratification that's all you have to make a lasting impression. A few seconds.

A great website can increase your business' revenue and bottom line. Building a website with a clear goal and strategy will help you to increase leads, sales, and ultimately help you grow your business. The internet never closes, people can access your website 24/7 from all over the world. Your website can handle thousands of customers at a time, it can take on multiple transactions, it doesn't get tired, it doesn't take days off, it doesn't call in sick. It's always working for you, even while you sleep. So why would you skimp out on something so detrimental to your business?

Sadly, lots of companies drop to ball here. The # 1 excuse I've always heard is due to price. A great website does not come cheap. But when you think of how much potential business you could lose due to your website, isn't this where you would want to spend some money? Your website is the foundation of your online presence. How much business do you think you would get if you didn't shower, didn't wash your clothes, didn't brush your teeth and yet greeted customers at the door when they walked up to your business. How many of them would want to do business with you? My guess is not many. Think of your website the same way. You want it to be clean, polished, and professional.

Your website works as a constant marketing representative that helps new people learn about your business. Potential customers can access your website whenever they want to access it day or night. This is great for your business because customers have different work schedules, different sleep schedules, and different social schedules.

In today's digital world people aren't only looking for things while your business is open Monday – Friday 9am-5pm. Those days are long gone. Having a strong online presence is great for your business because your company is always available. They can check out your business, your portfolio, read your reviews, etc. without having to wait for your normal operating business hours. Also, they don't have to get dressed, get in the car, fight traffic, look of parking, just to come down and talk about getting a new pool put in.

Here are the top 16 key elements of a high-quality website that you should be sure to consider:

1. Relevance and context

Developing well written and informative content for the user is one of the best factors in creating a high-quality website. Quality content is original, purposeful, and correctly optimized information that people, and search engines are driven to read, view, and share. According to Search Metrics, Google's algorithm recognizes high quality, relevant content, and rewards it with higher rankings. Focus on creating only the best high-quality content that you can. It will help you rank better and delight your potential customers.

2. Grammar and spelling

Why would a search engine show a page of content with grammar and spelling errors higher in the rankings when other pages of error free content exist? The answer: They won't! Grammar and spelling mistakes make you look bad in the eyes of your customer, and the search engines may even penalize you for it. Always read your copy at least 2 times before you publish it or hire an editor to proofread and edit your post if you need help. Flawless copy makes your website look professional and will earn you better rankings.

3. Readability

Readability is the ease in which text can be read and understood. Use shorter sentences, paragraphs, and active web forms. Remove all clutter, unnecessary words and limit the use of adverbs and adjectives.

4. Formatting

79% of users always scan web pages, according to a Nielsen study. Not only that but visitors are less likely to read a post with poor formatting. High quality content is easier to read, and suitable for scanning and skimming. Use **H1, H2, H3, etc. tags, number lists, and bullet points** to break down your content. Keep sentences and paragraphs short. Use **bold** and *italics* to highlight important parts so that they are highly visible as people scan.

5. Images and video

Include images or videos in every piece of content that you publish. Web pages with images and videos are more engaging for visitors and rank better in Google too (according to Search Metrics). Keep in mind that web pages in top rankings have an average of 7 images on their page so be sure to use at least a few.

6. Expertise

High quality pages and websites need enough expertise to be authoritative and trustworthy on their topic. The expertise of the author is a critical factor for any content to be considered high quality. People want to read posts from experts that can dig into a topic and explain it. Focus on writing detailed, well-researched posts and give examples to support your points.

7. Social media shares

High quality websites have social media buttons present on their pages.

Place your social media sharing icons visibly on the page and include call-to-action for people to share.

8. Internal and external links

Linking to valuable internal and external resources not only delights your readers but will also help you rank better. 9 out of 10 sites at position 1 in the Search Engine Results Page have at least one internal self-referencing link. Focus on building a nice internal link architecture. The URL that you link to and the anchor text need to be relevant to your content. Never link to unrelated pages or you may be penalized by Google and it leads to poor user experience overall.

9. Customer service that's easily accessible

If someone visiting your site has a question or problem, they shouldn't have to hunt for customer service options. This should be readily available. When customer service is unreachable, it makes the visitor feel uneasy. Especially if it's during normal business hours. Adding a FAQ's page will help to minimize phone calls for simple questions.

10. All your contact information

This should go without saying, but you'd be surprised how often I can't find contact information on websites. When I see that, I think it's sketchy. What are they trying to hide by withholding their phone number? Make sure your site has:

- physical address
- email address
- phone number
- links to social pages (Facebook, Instagram, YouTube, LinkedIn)

Failure to do so will make your page appear untrustworthy.

11. Reviews and testimonials

Showcasing customer testimonials on your website helps generate Social proof. This is especially true if you can get a testimonial from an expert in your industry. You should also have a place on your site where customers can leave reviews.

While good reviews are obviously what you're looking for, some unfavorable comments may actually boost your credibility as well. If all customer feedback on your website is positive, it may appear fake. Even if some people didn't have the best experience with your business, allowing them to leave a review for others to read will establish trust. It also helps prove you're an actual business and not a scam. Interact with the customers who left a review on your site. This will help build credibility as well.

12. Validation from other media sources

Have you been featured in a magazine, newspaper, or on another website? Any positive press about your company should be proudly displayed on your site. If established media sources have verified your business, it will increase your legitimacy in the eyes of anyone who visits your website. Find a good spot on your page to add any videos, screenshots, or links to all those stories.

13. Awards and achievements

Your website is a great place to show off any awards or achievements. Whether it's local, regional, or national, anything helps. Even if you won an award a couple of years ago, put it up on your website. Showcasing awards from the past shows you've been credible for a while. It establishes your company's history over time. Companies that have been in business for longer periods tend to be well established and appear more credible than those that just started. If you've been operating since 1950, don't be afraid to plaster that fact on your website.

14. Ease of navigation

Customers shouldn't struggle to find what they're looking for on your website. The menu options should be limited so it's not too overwhelming. Adding a search bar so your readers can look for something specific is a great way to improve your navigation as well. All of this helps enhance the user experience, which helps with your credibility score.

15. Page loading speed

The faster your page loads, the higher your conversion rates will be.

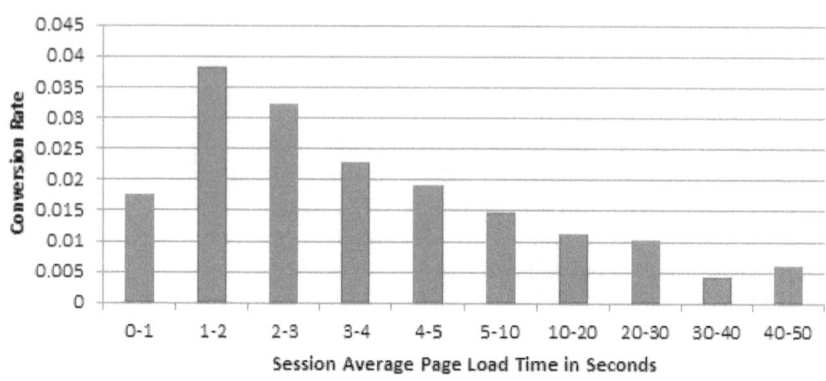

Conversion Rate by Page Load Time

It's that simple. Don't try to find the cheapest web hosting service on the market. You get what you pay for. It's worth it to pay a little extra to avoid technical glitches and always have fast loading times.

16. Clearly state all policies

Don't assume website visitors know your company policies. All of these should be clearly stated on your website. This will help you from a legal perspective as well in case there is a dispute.

I wish I could tell you that if you just picked a few of the key elements above, you'd have a great website. But the reality is, you won't. It's a total package type of thing, and you need to work on all of the elements listed above. Sure, implementing a few of them is better than implementing none, but the goal is to make your website so great that people trust you and want to buy from you. If your site looks incomplete or untrustworthy, it can drastically impact your traffic and conversions. Make sure you do your best to create a high-quality website by using as many of the 16 key elements that we described above.

If after reading this Chapter you feel like your website just isn't up to par with what it should be. You can contact at us at www.PoolBuilderMarketingPROS.com We can help!

Chapter 3 Key Points

- Your company's website is often your first impression you give to potential customers and helps to establish credibility.

- Building a website with a clear goal and strategy will help you to increase leads, sales, and ultimately help you grow your business.

- Quality content is original, purposeful, and correctly optimized information that people, and search engines are driven to read, view, and share

- Web pages with images and videos are more engaging for visitors and rank better in Google too (according to Search Metrics).

- Place your social media sharing icons visibly on the page and include call-to-action for people to share.

- Never link to unrelated pages or you may be penalized by Google and it leads to poor user experience overall.

- While good reviews are obviously what you're looking for, some unfavorable comments may actually boost your credibility as well.

- The faster your page loads, the higher your conversion rates will be.

- If your site looks incomplete or untrustworthy, it can drastically impact your traffic and conversions.

Chapter 4
SEARCH ENGINE OPTIMIZATION (SEO)

Search engine optimization is the process of getting your business to show up on the search engines such as Google, Bing, and Yahoo as customers are searching for your services. Think of the search engines like you would Real Estate. Location, Location, Location. The best spots on page #1 of the search engines is Prime Real Estate. It's become more and more important over the last decade as customers have been making the transition from Newspapers, Yellow pages, and Billboards to online medias. Google alone averages 40,000 searches every second, which equates to 1.2 trillion searches worldwide per year.

Google remains the most popular search engine. Google was launched on September 15, 1997 based on a simple algorithm. The funny thing about algorithms is that they don't care if you have the best product, who you are, or if you have the best customer service. All they care about is if your website meets their certain criteria, and if it does, they will rank it higher than websites that don't. Period.

SEO refers to getting your business's website to show up in the organic & map listings. These listings account for a majority of the search volume. More than 78% of searches click on the organic (non-paid listings) rather than the paid listings. When it comes to SEO and Online Marketing for Pool Builders there three very critical components of Search Engine Marketing that must be understood. These three components are:

- **Paid Listings** – The area along the top that advertisers can bid on & pay to obtain placement in the search engines.
- **Map Listings** – These are the listings that come up underneath the paid listings.
- **Organic Listings** – The area in the body of the search engine results page.

So, what can you do to get your business's website to show up in the organic section of a search engine? This starts with optimizing your website (remember your website is the foundation of your online presence) for placement in the organic section:

- Make sure to do the necessary SEO optimization work on each of your pages and update the Title Tags, include keywords in the URL, use keywords in the H1 Tag and throughout the body and use anchor text with keywords that you want to optimize for the navigation.
- Submit your sitemap with all the pages to Google & Bing Webmaster tools via an XML file to ensure Google, Bing and Yahoo add your site & all of its pages to the index.
- Get Links! The site that has the most quality links will get top placement for the desired keywords.

Recently search engines have changed significantly; especially with the introduction of the Google map listings (Google Places) to the search results for local searches. The majority of Pool Contractors we talk with are confused about how the whole search engine thing works and the differences between paid, map, and organic listings. We are going to try and break it all down for you by understanding how each component works so you can formulate a strategy to maximize your results of each.

Paid / Pay Per Click Listings:

We'll be going over PPC more in depth in the next chapter but for SEO sake here's a brief overview of what PPC is. PPC or Pay Per Click is a great option for Pool Contractors because you can reach more qualified leads that are more likely to convert. When you utilize PPC you have complete control over your campaign. How it looks, how long it runs, who you want to see it, etc. You set a budget and bid on keywords that are relevant to you and pay to get listed in this area.

One of the great features of PPC is that you only pay when someone clicks on your ad. You don't pay for impressions or a monthly fee. The PPC system is based on a bidding system and the company that bids the highest gets the best placement. PPC is a great way to get your business in front of qualifies buys but should be thought of as a short-term solution to get instant leads coming in.

Map Listings:

The map listings have become very important recently since it is the first thing that comes up in the search results for most locally based searches. If someone searches "Pool Builder + your city" the chances are that the map listings will be the first thing they look at. Unlike the paid section of the search engine, you can't buy your way in to the map listings, you have to earn it, and once you do, there is no cost per click as associated like with being in the paid section of the search engines. Getting your business on the Google Places Map Listing is a MUST for any local Pool Builder Business, it's the very first thing potential customers see. Even above the Organic results.

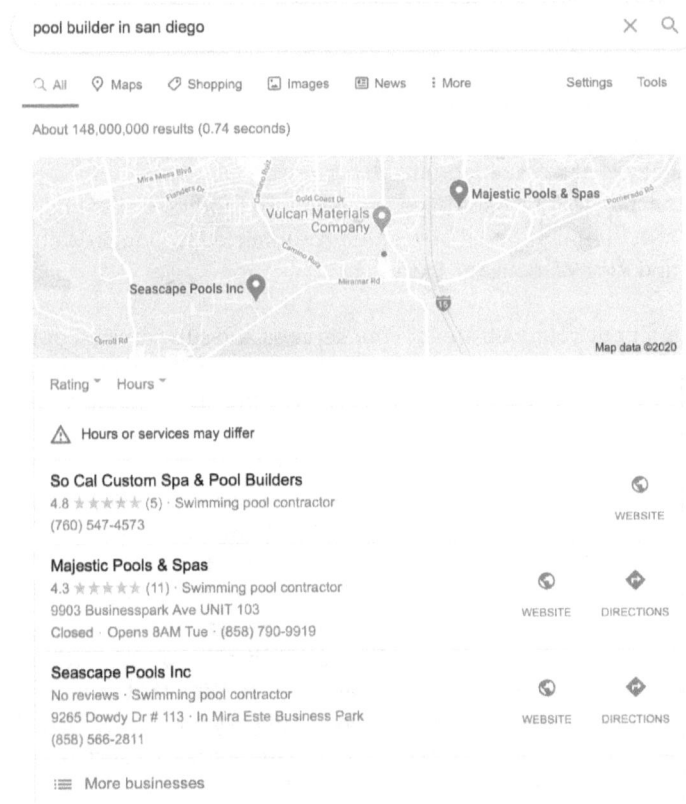

Organic Listings:

The Organic section of the search engine results page appears directly beneath the map listings in many local searches but appears directly beneath the paid listings in the absence of the map listings (the map section only shows up in specific local searches). Similar to the map listings, you can't buy your way into this section of the search engines and there is no cost per click as associated with the paid section. You have to earn your top spot in this section. This takes constant maintenance to get here, and to maintain your top spot. Again, this all starts with your website and how well it's built and optimized from an SEO perspective. Here are some of the most important items that need to be taken care of for on-page search engine optimization:

- URL should contain page keyword
- Unique Title Tag on each page
- H1 Tag re-stating that Title Tag on each Page
- Images named with primary keywords
- Anchor Text on each page and built into footer – Dallas Pool Builder
- XML Sitemap should be created & submitted to Google Webmaster Tools and Bing Webmaster Tools

If you built out your website for your services and sub-services, optimize the pages using SEO best practices and then systematically obtain inbound links to those pages and sub-pages, you will start to rank higher in the search engines for Pool Builder related keywords.

Now that you understand the three major components of the search engine results and the differences between paid listings, map listings, and organic listings you might be asking yourself… "What section is the most important?" We get asked this question a lot by Pool Builders all over the country. The fact is that all three components are important, and each should have a place in your online marketing program. You want to show up as often as possible when someone is searching for a Pool Builder in your service area. With that said, assuming you are operating on a limited budget and need to make your marketing dollars stretch as far as possible: you need to focus your investment on the sections that are going to drive the strongest return on investment.

Research shows that the vast majority of the population look directly at the organic and map listings when searching and their eyes simply glance over the paid ad listings. So, if you're operating on a limited budget and need to get the best bang for your buck, you should start by focusing your efforts on the area that gets the most clicks at the lowest cost. We have found that placement in the organic and map sections on the search engines drive a significant better return on investment than Pay Per Click marketing does.

Here's a list of some of the best SEO tools for beginners:

1. Screaming Frog SEO Spider
2. Click Web Analytics
3. Proranktracker
4. SEMrush
5. Google Search Console
6. Pagespeed Insights
7. Redirect Path
8. Majestic
9. Answer The Public
10. Google Analytics

If after reading this Chapter you feel like your website may not be optimized for the search engines. Or you want our help getting to the top. You can contact us at www.PoolBuilderMarketingPROS.com We can help!

Chapter 4 Key Points

- It's become more and more important over the last decade as customers have been making the transition from Newspapers, Yellow pages, and Billboards to online medias.

- More than 78% of searches click on the organic (non-paid listings) rather than the paid listings.

- The PPC system is based on a bidding system and the company that bids the highest gets the best placement.

- Getting your business on the Google Places Map Listing is a MUST for any local Pool Builder Business, it's the very first thing potential customers see. Even above the Organic results.

- If you built out your website for your services and sub-services, optimize the pages using SEO best practices and then systematically obtain inbound links to those pages and sub-pages, you will start to rank higher in the search engines for Pool Builder related keywords.

CHAPTER 5
PAY - PER- CLICK (PPC) MARKETING

As we discussed previously. Pay-per-click (PPC) is the marketing model that lets you place ads on an ad platform and pay the host of that platform every time your ad is clicked. The goal of a PPC ad is to lead the person viewing it to click through to your website, where that visitor can complete a valuable action, such as purchasing your product or scheduling a bid. There are several platforms that offer PPC advertising.

Here's a list of some platforms you may have heard of that all offer PPC advertising

- Google Ads
- Bing Ads
- Yahoo Gemini
- Facebook
- LinkedIn
- Twitter
- Pinterest
- Instagram
- YouTube

With Google owning over 75% of the search market share, this is who we will use as an example in this Chapter. Search engines are incredibly popular advertising platforms. They allow you to display ads that are relevant to what users are searching for. Search engines like Google AdWords and Bing Ads operate with real-time bidding (RTB), where advertising inventory is sold in a private automated auction using real-time data.

There are four distinct benefits to PPC marketing:

1. **Speed -** You can quickly drive a significant amount of traffic to your website. If managed effectively, PPC marketing is one of the fastest digital marketing strategies to drive traffic and conversion growth.

2. **Precision** - Creating a highly-targeted audience to show your ads to is straightforward—especially on Search and Shopping Networks.

3. **Agility** - Performance data is available almost immediately, which makes it easier to quickly make adjustments to improve your chances for a successful campaign.

4. **Measurement** - With effective conversion tracking, advertisers can see the return on investment of their ads.

While there are distinct advantages to PPC, the advertising model does come with potential pitfalls under the wrong management you should be aware of.

1. **Cost** - Depending on your competition and your service area, PPC marketing can be very expensive. Some ad placements can cost over $100 per click! (Don't worry, this isn't common, but it does show the variability of the PPC market due to its auction model.)

2. **Waste** - Due to the technical nature of most PPC platforms, wasted ad spend is common for businesses who don't know exactly what they are doing. That's why we don't suggest trying this out yourself and leaving it to us to handle for you.

3. **Volume** - PPC marketing, especially on the Search Network, often depends on search volume. If users aren't searching for the product or service you offer, Search and Shopping ads won't generate much traffic.

If you have a website, (which we have already discussed in Chapter 3) and you should. You have to consider PPC advertising as a marketing channel. Just because you have a website does not mean that everyone you want to see it is going to come just because it's there. You should engage in PPC (for the short term anyway), until your SEO is working, and you are at the top of the search engines in your area.

Before starting your first PPC marketing campaign, consider your budget, advertising goals, competition, and risk tolerance:

1. Do you have a clear conversion goal? PPC advertising is most effective when you can match dollars spent to a conversion like a transaction or lead form completion. Clear conversion goals help you do that.

2. What are you trying to accomplish? PPC is great for responsive, nimble advertising. But when you stop spending, PPC stops producing. If you want to balance this with earned media, we always suggest adding SEO to the mix.

3. How much can you spend on PPC before you get a return on investment? Reality check: Your ads won't produce instant results. Be ready to spend some money without a return. It might be $50 or $10,000. Just have a number in mind.

PPC marketing works on an auction system like eBay. You literally pick up the keywords that you want to show up for and bid what you would be willing to pay for each click. There are a number of factors that determine placement which we will be discussing further in understanding the Ad auction process but at the broadest sense, the pool contractor who is willing to pay the most per click will be at the top position and the second most will be in the second position etc.

PPC marketing is a great way to get your business on the top of the search engines right away and start driving qualified traffic to your website. As explained earlier in the book, we feel that you will get a better return on investment from organic placement, and a good SEO strategy but if you really want to dominate your service area running a PPC campaign on Google Ad words or Bing search will give you additional exposure online and can generate a solid return on investment when managed properly.

In the paid section of the search engines you are able to select the keywords that are relevant to you and then pay to be listed in this area. The reason it is referred to PPC or Pay Per Click is because rather than paying a flat monthly fee for placement, you simply pay each time someone clicks on the link. The PPC platform is based on a bidding system like an auction and the company that bids the highest gets the best placement.

Many people believe that your position in the sponsored listings is driven exclusively by your bid price. There are actually several variables that come into play in addition to bid price to determine where your ad will appear in the sponsored listings:

- Max Bid Price - this is the max bid for a given search term – set by you.
- Quality score – is determined by Google based on a number of variables
  1. Being click through rate.
  2. Relevance.
  3. Quality of you landing page

Your Max Bid Price X You Quality Score = Your Ad Rank.
Ad Rank is the position in which you will appear in the listings.

The next question is how is your cost per click determined? With Google you only pay as much as the maximum bid of the bidder directly beneath you in the bidding auction. Ultimately it is Ad Rank of advertiser below / quality score of advertisers 1.
By increasing your quality score, you can actually reduce your cost per click and improve your position in the sponsored listings. Understanding how the ad words auction process works and helps us understand that we must both bid appropriately and make sure that our ad / pages are relevant.

Be sure that your keywords, text ads and landing pages are as relevant as possible. The best way to do this is to buy creating separate landing pages for each of your keyword categories or keywords. E.g. if you are bidding on "Las Vegas Pool Repair" then have a page on your website that is specific referring to "Las Vegas Pool Repair" and point the ad to that page. By doing so you will improve your quality score and reduce your cost per click

Getting started with PPC. In order to start a pay-per-click campaign you will need to set up a Google ad words account by going to www.google/adwords.

- Login with your Gmail account or create a new account.
- Click "Create AdWords Campaign".
- Google will then ask you a series of questions to determine what type of business you are and the type of services you are looking to promote.
- Fill in your campaign details.
- Be sure to set your target area in location and service area.
- Click on the "Extensions Link" and add

Location based on Google places listing - this will show your sponsored ad with a blue push pin in the map next to your listing. Call extension. This is so that you can place a unique phone number into the ad for a call tracking purposes. Your phone number will also show up on the ad itself and could possibly generate calls directly from the ad without a click or a FREE call.

In the next section Google will ask you to write your ad and select your keywords. For your ad be sure you have a clear call to action e.g. call us now for a quick service at 555-123-4567.

In the keywords section be sure to list each of your important services combined with / without the cities that you operate in.

Even if you use generic keywords like "Pool Builder", "Pool Contractor", "Pool Repair", etc. your ad will only be shown to those within your service area (as defined by you in step one). Google can do this by referring to the searchers IP address which shows their approximate location at the time of the search.

We do not recommend creating a generic ad for all of your keywords. Rather, create a different ad for each keyword combination and land it on a separate page of your website. By doing so you will have a better-quality score and will get you a lower cost per click for top positioning.

PPC is great for any kind of business whether large or small and having a PPC component to your marketing strategies will ensure that you capture your potential customers at the right time. When they are ready for that new pool. With PPC you can build your online marketing strategies to measure the much – optimized results. If you maintain and optimize your PPC campaigns frequently, you can be sure to benefit from getting qualifies can converting traffic to your website and your business.

If you follow the instructions in this chapter you will be able to set up a PPC campaign on Google and understand the underlying strategy involved in getting the lowest cost per click and the best conversion rate possible.

If after reading this Chapter you feel like you're not ready to tackle the world of PPC on you own or you want to advertise on one or several of the other platforms. You can contact us at www.PoolBuilderMarketingPROS.com We can help!

Chapter 5 Key Points

- The goal of a PPC ad is to lead the person viewing it to click through to your website, where that visitor can complete a valuable action, such as purchasing your product or scheduling a bid.

- Just because you have a website does not mean that everyone you want to see it is going to come just because it's there. You should engage in PPC (for the short term anyway), until your SEO is working, and you are at the top of the search engines in your area.

- PPC marketing is a great way to get your business on the top of the search engines right away and start driving qualified traffic to your website.

- By increasing your quality score, you can actually reduce your cost per click and improve your position in the sponsored listings.

- PPC is great for any kind of business whether large or small and having a PPC component to your marketing strategies will ensure that you capture your potential customers at the right time.

CHAPTER 6
RETARGETING ADS

How many times have you been on a website only to leave without buying anything? Then later you're on a completely different website looking at something else and an ad for what you were looking at earlier pops up. You have been Retargeted.

What is Retargeting and How Does it Work?

Retargeting, also known as remarketing, is a form of online marketing that can help you keep your brand in front of bounced traffic after they leave your website. For most websites, only 2% of website traffic converts on the first visit. Retargeting is a tool designed to help companies reach the 98% of users who don't convert right away.

How Does Retargeting Work?

Retargeting is a cookie-based technology that uses simple JavaScript code to anonymously 'follow' your audience all over the Web.

Here's how it works: you place a small, unobtrusive piece of code on your website (this code is sometimes referred to as a pixel). The code, or pixel, is unnoticeable to your site visitors and won't affect your site's performance. Every time a new visitor comes to your site, the code drops an anonymous browser cookie. Later, when your cookied visitors browse the Web, the cookie will let your retargeting provider know when to serve ads, ensuring that your ads are served to only to people who have previously visited your site.

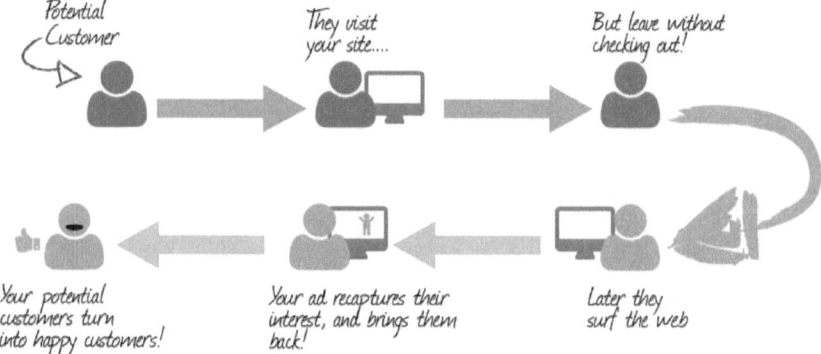

Retargeting is so effective because it focuses your advertising spend on people who are already familiar with your brand and have recently demonstrated interest. That's why most digital marketers who use it see a higher ROI than from most other digital channels.

When Does Retargeting Work?

Retargeting is a powerful branding and conversion optimization tool, but it works best if it's part of a larger digital marketing strategy.

Retargeting works best in conjunction with inbound and outbound marketing or demand generation. Strategies involving content marketing, AdWords, and targeted display are great for driving traffic, but they don't help with conversion optimization. Conversely, retargeting can help increase conversions, but it can't drive people to your site. Your best chance of success is using other tools like SEO, and PPC to drive traffic and retargeting to get the most out of that traffic.

Retargeting campaigns remind your website visitors of your products and services after they leave your website without buying. After visiting specific pages, it allows you to retarget them and show your visitors relevant visual or text ads when they visit other websites. Retargeting campaigns could be done with the help of Goodle Ads, Facebook retargeting, LinkedIn Ads and other retargeting platforms. Serious marketers today use retargeting as a vital tool to connect with their customers and increase their sales and customer loyalty.

Before someone decides to buy your product or service, they need to feel like they know you. A good marketing rule of thumb to help customers make up their mind about purchasing is to ensure they hear your message at least 7 times. Retargeting builds visibility for your brand, allowing you to reach an audience that has already expressed interest in your products.

When should you use retargeting campaigns?

- Retargeting is meant to be a long-term strategy for businesses that already have a following. If your website gets at least 100 monthly visitors, Google remarketing ads are definitely for you.
- Promoting bestsellers. Retargeting ads are a simple, effective way to showcase your top-selling products. And promoting items your current customers love can even help convert visitors into customers and increase ROI on your ads.
- Introducing new pool designs. People who are interested in your brand and visit your site are a great audience to target when you're launching a new product or pool design. Your retargeting ads will catch their eye wherever they go online, creating a clear path back to your store so they can check out what's new. This can be done with display campaigns using Google AdWords or through a Facebook retargeting campaign.
- Building brand awareness. Most people need to feel they know you before they decide to buy your product or service, and retargeting ads keep your brand top of mind for potential customers who aren't ready to purchase when they first visit your site.

Retargeting vs remarketing campaigns
"Retargeting" and "remarketing" are pretty similar as they mean to achieve the same goals:

- Target audiences who already visited your site and are aware of your brand
- Engage and target people who are most likely to make a purchase
- Help start building a lasting connection with the customers through brand awareness and recognition

The differences between retargeting vs. remarketing are in the tactics used to accomplish these goals.

Retargeting primarily uses paid ads to target audiences who have visited your website or Social Media profiles. Remarketing primarily uses email to target people who have already done business with your brand.

You need more than one Online Marketing channel to ensure none of your customers fall through the cracks. According to Google, combining retargeting with the other advertising you already do can help you sell 50% more stuff.

If you like to add a Retargeting element to your Online Marketing strategy. You can contact us at www.PoolBuilderMarketingPROS.com We can help!

Chapter 6 Key Points

- Retargeting, also known as remarketing, is a form of online marketing that can help you keep your brand in front of bounced traffic after they leave your website.

- Retargeting works best in conjunction with inbound and outbound marketing or demand generation.

- A good marketing rule of thumb to help customers make up their mind about purchasing is to ensure they hear your message at least 7 times.

- Most people need to feel they know you before they decide to buy your product or service, and retargeting ads keep your brand top of mind for potential customers who aren't ready to purchase when they first visit your site.

- Retargeting primarily uses paid ads to target audiences who have visited your website or Social Media profiles. Remarketing primarily uses email to target people who have already done business with your brand.

CHAPTER 7
SOCIAL MEDIA MARKETING

With the invention of Social Media, this isn't marketing anymore. It's more of psychology used as a tool to sell and monetize. AND IT WORKS!! Millions of people jump on Social Media every day to escape the realities of their everyday lives. People don't want to be sold to; they want to be engaged with. Society has shifted and so must your marketing tactics and strategies. The old ways of marketing are over.

Marketing and advertising need to be built on genuine communication not mass communication. The good news is that with digital marketing and Social Media marketing we can now target your dream demographic directly instead of wasting money and time just marketing to the masses and hoping that your dream customer sees your ads. Back in 2010 there weren't even a billion people using Social Media, now that number has grown to almost 3 billion over the last 10 years.

With so many Social Media sites out there where should you be? Well let's go over some of them so you can narrow down on where you should be focusing on.

24 Social Media Sites You Need to Know in 2020

#1: Facebook

Despite a tumultuous 2018, Facebook is still the top social network in the United States, with over 2.7 billion monthly active users as of the second quarter of 2020, Facebook is the biggest social network worldwide. The company's other properties Instagram and Facebook Messenger ranked second and third with over a billion and 1.3 billion users respectively. In the third quarter of 2012, the number of active Facebook users surpassed one billion, making it the first social network ever to do so. Active users are those which have logged in to Facebook during the last 30 days. During the last reported quarter, the company stated that 3.14 billion people were using at least one of the company's core products (Facebook, WhatsApp, Instagram, or Messenger) each month.

#2: Instagram

As of July 2020, 33.8 percent of global Instagram audiences were aged between 25 and 34 years. In total, over two thirds of total Instagram audiences were aged 34 years and younger and this makes the platform particularly attractive for marketers. With over 1 billion active users, Instagram belongs to the most popular social networks worldwide. The social photo sharing app is especially popular in the United States, India, and Brazil, which have over 130 million, 100 and 91 million Instagram users each. In the United States, the number on Instagram users is projected to surpass 130 million Monthly Active Users in 2022.

#3 Facebook Messenger

Facebook Messenger has over 1.3 billion users globally and is expected to grow to 2.4 billion users by 2021. More than 20 billion messages are exchanged between business and users monthly on Facebook Messenger. There are more than 300,000 active chat bots on Messenger. Messenger marketing leads to 70% better open rate than email marketing.

#4: YouTube

YouTube is the largest video-sharing social media site in the world with over 2 billion monthly active users worldwide. It lets users upload videos on the platform, view videos from other users, and interact with them. 62% of businesses use YouTube as a channel to post video content. 90% of people say they discover new brands or products on YouTube. 400 hours of video content is uploaded to YouTube every minute worldwide. YouTube users spend an average of 40 minutes watching videos on the platform.

#5: Twitter

Twitter is a platform that lets users stay on top of trending topics and engage in relevant conversations. As of the first quarter of 2019, Twitter averaged 330 million monthly active users, a decline from its all-time high of 336 monthly active users in the first quarter of 2018. While Twitter doesn't have as many users as other top Social Media sites, it does have a highly engaged user base. Twitter users send out at least 500 million tweets per day on average.

#6: LinkedIn

Linked in

LinkedIn is a Social Media site geared more towards professionals and is very popular among B2B audiences. The platform has grown rapidly over the years and currently has 706 million members in 200 countries and regions worldwide. 189M+ just in North America. Members can expand their professional connections on the platform and showcase their portfolios. LinkedIn is also an excellent platform to share your professional expertise, as it allows members to publish blogs that reside on the platform.

#7: WhatsApp

WhatsApp is a cross-platform instant messaging service for smartphones that lets users shar text messages, images, voice notes, audio files, documents, and videos. As of March 2020, WhatsApp had two billion monthly active users, up from over 1 billion monthly active users in February 2016. The service is one of the most popular mobile messaging apps worldwide and was acquired by social network Facebook for 19 billion U.S. dollars in February 2014. Along with its growing user base, the platform has also introduced many new features to make interactions easier among users. While users could only make one-on-one calls before, it now had a group calling feature. They also introduced a WhatsApp Status feature that allows users to update photo, and text statuses that disappear after 24 hrs. As of Q1 of 2019, 500 million users were updating their WhatsApp status daily.

#8: Snapchat

Snapchat is another highly visual Social Media platform that's popular among the younger generation. Users can send "Snaps" to each other and update 24-hour statues just like on WhatsApp and Instagram. As of July 2020, photo and video sharing app Snapchat had 398 million monthly active users worldwide. With an estimated 46 million monthly active users in the United States, Snapchat easily ranks among the most popular social apps in the country.

#9: Pinterest

Pinterest is a virtual scrapbooking highly visual Social Media site. Users can create themed vision boards and add images and products to the board. Brands can even create Shoppable Pins through which users can directly make purchases. In 2019, there were 335 million monthly active users on the platform. These users have created more 200 billion pins on over 4 billion boards.

#10: Reddit

Formerly known as "the front page of the internet", Reddit is an online forum platform with over 130,000 sub-forums and communities. The platform allows registered users, called Redditors, to post content. Each post is open to the entire Reddit community to vote upon, either by down- or upvotes. The most popular posts are featured directly on the front page. Subreddits are available by category and Redditors can follow selected subreddits relevant to their interest and also control what content they see on their custom front page. Reddit is a web traffic powerhouse: in May 2020 over 1.5 billion visits were measured to the online forum, making it one of the most-visited websites online. The United States accounts for the biggest share of Reddit's desktop traffic, followed by the UK, and Canada. As of September 2019, Reddit ranked among the most popular mobile social apps in the US with almost 48 million monthly active users.

#11: Tumblr

Tumblr is another leading Social Media site. Users can join communities and participate in cultural dialogues to expand their ideas. It's one of the top Social Media sites for self-expression and is very popular among teens and fandoms. In February 2020, there were a total or 321 million unique visitors to the website.

#12: Yelp

Yelp is crowd-sourcing review website where users can share their opinions about local businesses. Yelp boasts an average of 92 million unique mobile users per month. Yelp has more than 178 million unique visitors monthly across mobile, desktop and app platforms. Up to 9% increase in revenue for every new star earned on Yelp. ... 35% of people searching on Yelp will make a visit to the site they check within 24 hours.

#13 Houzz

Houzz is a platform that connects homeowners with design and building professionals. Houzz's platform has disrupted the traditional way homeowners find and choose professionals—similar to how Facebook has disrupted the way we now stay connected to old acquaintances or people we barely know in "real life." Houzz is an online community, directory and market place for all things home design. Whether you are building a pool, remodeling a backyard, or just dreaming about it. Houzz offers a great deal of assistance and inspiration. Houzz has 40 million users and 1.5 million local professionals.

#14. TikTok

If you have kids in 2020 you most likely have heard of TikTok. TikTok is one of the fastest growing social media platforms in the world which presents an alternative version of online sharing. It allows users to create short videos with music, filters, and some other features. This app is famous for its lip-sync videos and has over 800 million monthly users.

#15. Vimeo

Vimeo is another video sharing social media platform like YouTube or Twitch. You can create and share videos or go live. Just like with the other video sharing platforms. Vimeo has about 240 million active monthly users. Because Vimeo is smaller and more niche, your videos have a better chance of being found and followed within their community driven platform. There is less competition than on YouTube and sometimes the quality over quantity is better.

#16: Nextdoor

Nextdoor is a private social network for dedicated neighborhoods. You can enter your street address and find a community of people living in your area. While it was previously just for neighborhoods in the U.S., it has now expanded to other parts of the world. You can now use it from the U.K., Germany, France, Italy, Australia, Sweden, and Denmark. This is where neighbors can ask for others recommendations like, who built your pool?

Image: Nextdoor

#17: Quora

Quora is one of the largest social networks for people to ask and answer questions about hundreds of topics and categories. This includes everything from language and career to mythology and marketing. As of 2018, Quora had 300 million monthly active users.

#18: Meetup

Meetup is a social media site that does exactly what its name says. It helps connect users with local groups to meet up with new people. Groups can organize events for like-minded people to get together. You can find groups in a wide range of categories including outdoors and adventure, swimming, tech, photography, language, and culture, music, and more. It is most popular in the U.S., which contributes to 51.67% of it's traffic.

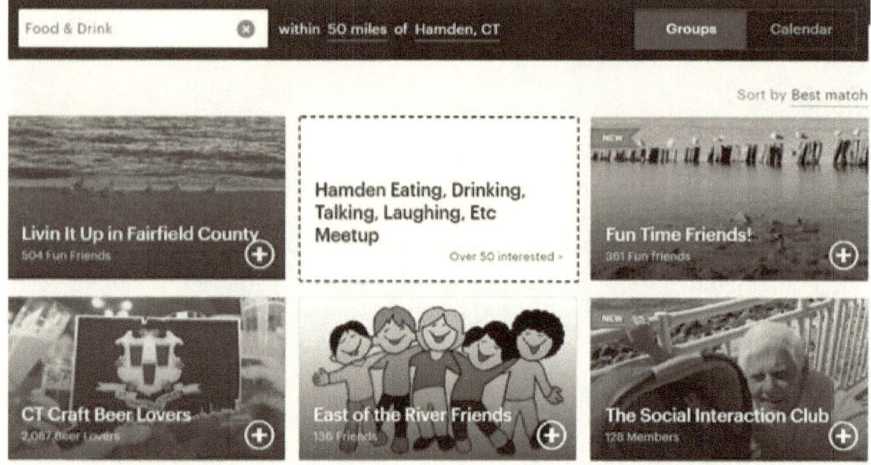

Image: Meetup

#19: Twitch

Twitch is the world's leading live streaming platform for gamers and the things they love. You can watch and chat now with millions of other fans from around the world. Users can interact with live streams from other gamers and comment on them or upload videos to Twitch for their audiences. It has about 6 million monthly steamers.

#20: Flickr

Flickr is another phot-sharing social media site that's a favorite among photographers and graphic designers. You can share original, high-quality images on the platform or discover relevant images from other users. You can also join groups and connect with new people with shared interests, like swimming pool designs.

#21: We Heart It

We Heart It describes itself as "A home for your inspiration" and a place to "Organize and share the things you love." Users can collect (or "**heart**") their favorite images to share with friends and organize into collections. Users can access the site through a web browser or We Heart It's iOS and Android mobile apps.

#22. Zoom

Zoom is the leader in modern enterprise video communications, with an easy, reliable cloud-based platform for video and audio conferencing, collaboration, chat, and webinars across mobile devices, desktops, telephones, and room systems.

#23. Foursquare Swarm

Foursquare has more than 55 million monthly active users. The Foursquare Swarm app has an average of 9 million daily check-ins and Foursquare has over 3 billion global visits monthly. Foursquare is a search and discovery-based app that helps users discover nearby places by providing recommendations. Foursquare is much more than a social media platform but is also a location data and technology platform

#24. Myspace

:::myspace

No, Myspace isn't dead. Myspace is one of the older social networking platforms and was the largest social platform almost a decade ago and was extremely popular in the U.S. The rise of other platforms like Facebook and Twitter led to a decline in its popularity. However, Myspace is still active and gets monthly traffic of over 7.5 million users. The main focus of the platform is on music now, but it is quite popular for blogs.

If after reading this chapter, you are still confused about where you should be and how to manage your Social Media presence. You can contact us at www.PoolBuilderMarketingPROS.com We can help!

Chapter 7 Key Points

- People don't want to be sold to; they want to be engaged with. Society has shifted and so must your marketing tactics and strategies. The old ways of marketing are over.

- Facebook is the biggest social network worldwide. The company's other properties Instagram and Facebook Messenger ranked second and third with over a billion and 1.3 billion users respectively.

- In the United States, the number on Instagram users is projected to surpass 130 million Monthly Active Users in 2022.

- 400 hours of video content is uploaded to YouTube every minute worldwide. YouTube users spend an average of 40 minutes watching videos on the platform.

- While Twitter doesn't have as many users as other top Social Media sites, it does have a highly engaged user base. Twitter users send out at least 500 million tweets per day on average.

- Reddit is a web traffic powerhouse: in May 2020 over 1.5 billion visits were measured to the online forum, making it one of the most-visited websites online.

- Yelp has more than 178 million unique visitors monthly across mobile, desktop and app platforms. Up to 9% increase in revenue for every new star earned on Yelp. ... 35% of people searching on Yelp will make a visit to the site they check within 24 hours.

Chapter 8
REVIEWS AND WHY THEY ARE IMPORTANT

Reviews are essential for your business and the future of your sales. With people now adays having such easy access to the web right in their pocket at all times, this has drastically changed the way people shop for almost everything today. From Pools to Landscaping, it's rare to blindly make a purchase decision without reading through several Online reviews. Research shows that 91% of people regularly or occasionally read online reviews, and 84% trust online reviews as much as a personal recommendation. And they make that decision quickly: 68% form an opinion after reading between one and six online reviews.

This means that whatever your industry, having a positive online presence gives you several key advantages, which is why it's becoming a key part of branding. Understanding why you need Online reviews will help you optimize your customer experience to help create a positive online footprint. Let's review some reasons why your consumers' published experiences with your brand are vital.

Social Proof Drives Purchases:

We're more likely to make a purchase if others around us, even total stranger agree that it is a good decision. Today, Online reviews are the biggest source of social proof, and they have a clear impact on sales. It's always a good strategy to encourage reviews by emailing customers after purchase and offering a special or discount coupon in return for a completed review. Customer feedback creates that 'social-proof' trust that encourages other potential customers to buy from you.

Reviews Make You More Visible:

Being a successful brand also means you're a visible one. Most shoppers will look on search engines like Google, Bing, and Yahoo or even on Social Media channels like Facebook, Instagram, YouTube when deciding who to buy a Pool from. These websites all have their own unique ways of indexing and surfacing content, but they all value original and fresh content, and customer reviews can definitely help feed the content machine, keeping your brand favored by algorithms. This will help to boost your SEO placement.

Having good Online customer reviews gives you a steady pipeline of positive content that search engines value highly when choosing which results to return. When you're ranked higher, algorithms and people alike tend to see your website as an authority in your industry, which also leads to more exposure.

Reviews Make You Look Trustworthy:

Your brand can build significant trust and credibility from a steady stream of positive reviews. One of the more interesting findings of recent research is just how powerful reviews are at building your company's online identity. Many shoppers distrust businesses that have ratings below (or even above) four stars. This leaves a small margin of error at the top, but companies with better average ratings are significantly more likely to see views converted to traffic and sales. The way customers are talking about you is just as important as the fact that they're saying your name. Having a highly positive footprint will eventually help you drive more sales.

Reviews Expand the Conversation About You:

Have you ever heard the saying "There's no such thing as bad press" Well this is partly true, unless it's all bad. Then you're screwed. The notion that all mentions in the media aid your cause of brand awareness, even if it's put into bad light. If you have all great reviews it seems fake to some people. We aren't saying to purposely not go for 5 stars on every job. But if you get a not so great review it's not the end of the world. Very good (or bad) reviews have a way of quickly spreading. Encouraging consumers to review your company is an easy way to expand your brand's reach.

When people have good things to say, they are also more likely to share their reviews on more sites, including external websites like Yelp, Google, and Facebook. These hubs are vital to your online presence, as Google collects data from their sites when building its own results ranking. Reviews on your website are always useful, but happy customers are likely to share their thoughts on as many places as possible, increasing your multi-channel footprint.

Reviews Are Increasingly Essential to Decision Making:

A proactively cultivated brand is one that increases your online visibility, and today, that means encouraging several ways for people to talk about you. Social media is a great tool, but the ability for customers to talk about you on other channels is a crucial component of your presence. By focusing on creating a steady stream of reviews, your brand is more likely to show up when customers are making their next major home decision.

Reviews Have a Clear Impact on Sales:

Case studies and theory can be misleading. Reality doesn't always follow a logic, and there are always outliers. But there's a growing body of benchmark data that proves that reviews do empirically lead to increased revenue. 88% of customers put as much weight on online reviews as they would on personal recommendations. Word-of-mouth has consistently been a critical consideration when it comes to a business' credibility. However, with the widespread accessibility of the internet today, online reviews now carry as much credibility as a personal recommendation from someone you know. The important thing to remember here is that consumers will trust a review that is both high-quality and authentic. If it seems spammy or paid for, it's likely to have the opposite effect and turn customers off.

Reviews Give You an Open Line to Consumers:

More than simply posting reviews, consumers today expect companies to respond to their comments. These reviews also give you a forum to be frank with consumers and reinforce positive reviews with thanks, or promotions. More importantly, they also give you a way to quickly rectify a poor review and show that you care. The immediacy of reviews and the personalized responses also mean that they give your brand a face. Having a friendly, open-to-feedback appearance can work wonders for your brand.

Remember You're Always Under Review

The way you market your brand is important, but having people talk about you is a great way to enhance your message. By encouraging positive conversations about your brand, you can quickly and clearly improve your marketing efforts.

If after reading this Chapter you feel like you could use some help with your Reputation management. You can contact us at www.PoolBuilderMarketingPROS.com We can help!

Chapter 8 Key Points

- Research shows that 91% of people regularly or occasionally read online reviews, and 84% trust online reviews as much as a personal recommendation. And they make that decision quickly: 68% form an opinion after reading between one and six online reviews.

- When you're ranked higher, algorithms and people alike tend to see your website as an authority in your industry, which also leads to more exposure.

- Social media is a great tool, but the ability for customers to talk about you on other channels is a crucial component of your presence.

- The immediacy of reviews and the personalized responses also mean that they give your brand a face. Having a friendly, open-to-feedback appearance can work wonders for your brand.

CHAPTER 9
CONCLUSION

We hope you got some good insight out of this book and have a better understanding of the wonderful world of Online Marketing. We have been helping companies like yours for a very long time and we take pride in what we do. We decided to write this book to help Pool Builders and the Swimming Pool Industry as a whole understand more about Online Marketing. We don't know how to build pools; we spend all our time in front of computers researching the always changing world of Online Marketing. These platforms change and evolve all the time and in order for us to continuously get you the best ROI on your marketing dollars that's just what we do.

If you've finished this book and still feel like you need some extra help navigating the online marketing world we are here to help. As the experts in the Swimming Pool Industry we have had tremendous success implementing our marketing tactics and strategies in the space and can help you along the way. Our team can review your present online presence and marketing initiatives and help set up a strategy to get you the absolute best return on your investment.

We are always here to help and you can contact us directly on our website at
www.PoolBuilderMarketingPROS.com

We look forward to helping you and growing our industry and creating new jobs for our society and our economy.

Thank you for taking the time to read our book. We hope you enjoyed it as much as we enjoyed putting it down on paper.

CHAPTER 10
RESOURCES

https://www.bing.com/

https://www.dailymail.co.uk/ushome/index.html

https://digitalmarketinginstitute.com/

https://dixa.com/

https://www.entrepreneur.com/

https://expandedramblings.com/

https://www.facebook.com/

https://www.flickr.com/

https://www.forbes.com/

https://www.google.com/

https://www.hobo-web.co.uk/

https://www.houzz.com/

https://influencermarketinghub.com/

https://www.instagram.com/

https://www.juicer.io/

https://www.linkedin.com/

https://mailchimp.com/

https://www.marketingprofs.com/

https://www.meetup.com/

https://mention.com/en/

https://www.messenger.com/

https://myspace.com/

https://nextdoor.com/

https://www.oberlo.com/

https://www.pinterest.com/

https://www.plumberseo.net/

https://www.prnewswire.com/

https://www.quicksprout.com/

https://www.quora.com/

https://www.reddit.com/

https://retargeter.com/

https://review42.com/

https://www.searchenginejournal.com/

https://www.similarweb.com/

https://www.snapchat.com/

https://www.statista.com/

https://www.swarmapp.com/

https://successwise.com/

https://www.tiktok.com/

https://www.tumblr.com/

https://www.twitch.tv/

https://twitchtracker.com/

https://twitter.com/

https://variety.com/

https://vimeo.com/

https://www.webfx.com/

https://www.whatsapp.com/

https://www.yahoo.com/

https://www.yelp.com/

https://www.youtube.com/

https://www.zoom.us/

Thank You